T0197426

TEACH THE CHILDREN
HOW TO BECOME
AN ASTRONAUT

BY DR. SUNSHINE

AuthorHouse™
1663 Liberty Drive
Bloomington, IN 47403
www.authorhouse.com
Phone: 833-262-8899

Because of the dynamic nature of the Internet, any web addresses or links contained in this book may have changed since publication and may no longer be valid. The views expressed in this work are solely those of the author and do not necessarily reflect the views of the publisher, and the publisher hereby disclaims any responsibility for them.

This book is printed on acid-free paper.

ISBN: 978-1-6655-6805-0 (sc)
ISBN: 978-1-6655-7492-1 (hc)
ISBN: 978-1-6655-6806-7 (e)

Print information available on the last page.

Published by AuthorHouse 11/02/2022

authorHOUSE®

TEACH THE CHILDREN HOW TO BECOME AN ASTRONAUT

If you want to be an astronaut you should go and see an air force recruiting officer to be an air force pilot to fly planes around.

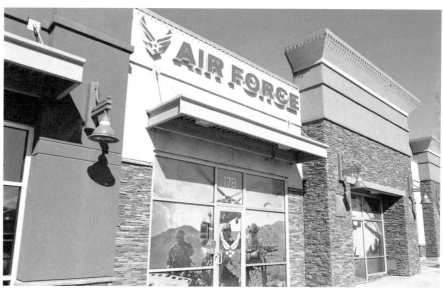

After you do join the air force you will feel that you're apart of
something that is very important.

After you learn how to fly a plane then you could be stationed on an aircraft carrier to keep the waters safe for the people around the world and after your tour of duty then you could maybe become an astronaut and could fly through the galaxy.

After your tour of duty with the air force on an aircraft carrier you can go and see a NASA recruiting officer to become an astronaut and to fly around in outer space.

After your tour of duty then you could become an astronaut and then you can fly to the moon and then around in space to check out the galaxy.

We're flying to the moon and we will be going to the space station.

You could fly around in space and work on the space station.

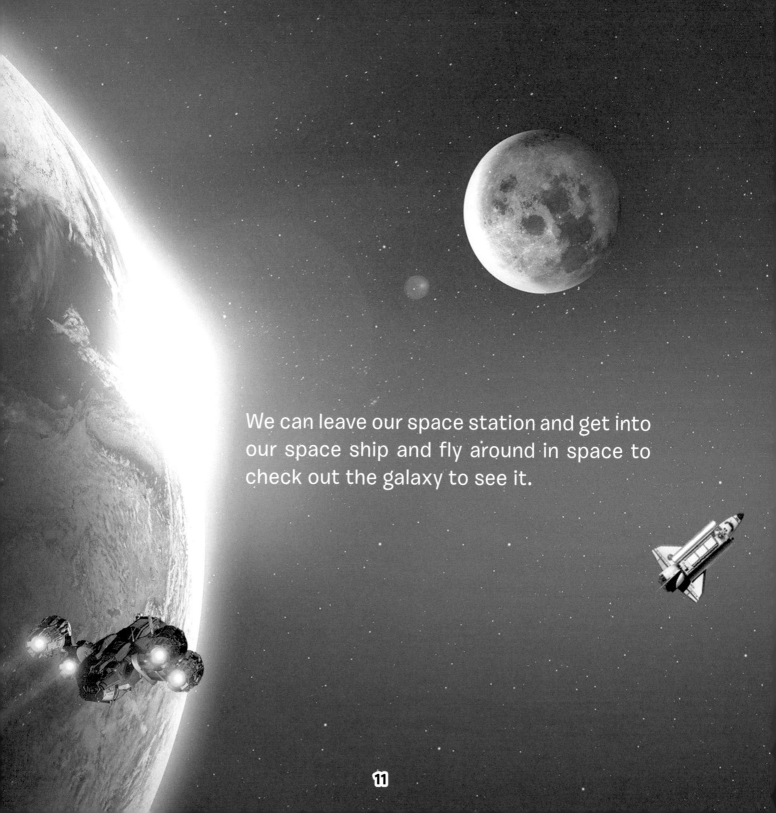

We can leave our space station and get into our space ship and fly around in space to check out the galaxy to see it.

We can just fly around in space
and check it out.

We can fly to this planet and get some rest and get something to eat and to continue to check out this galaxy.

We flew to our space station and now we are walking around and checking out our flag on this planet.

We can fly around in space and check it out and go into our space ship and fly around in the galaxy.

20

We can fly around to this next
planet and check it out.

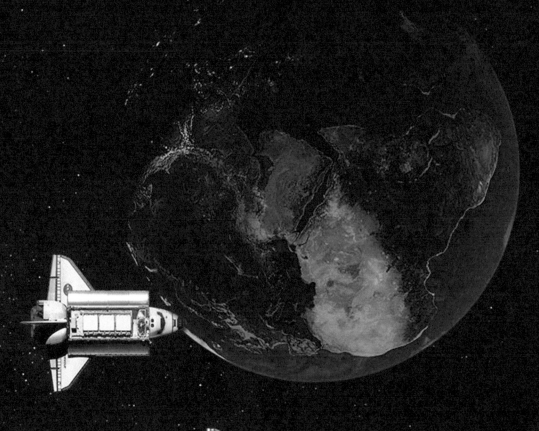

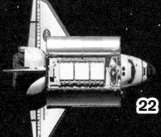

22

We flew to this planet and we are putting our flag on this planet to declare that we own this planet.

23

After we checked out this planet and we put our flag on it we're going to fly in our space ship and go home to our planet.

26

We're flying in our space ship to go back home to our planet earth.

Printed in the United States
by Baker & Taylor Publisher Services